Kathleen Kennedy

Movie Producer

by Kate Moening

BLASTOFF! READERS
2

BELLWETHER MEDIA • MINNEAPOLIS, MN

Note to Librarians, Teachers, and Parents:

Blastoff! Readers are carefully developed by literacy experts and combine standards-based content with developmentally appropriate text.

Level 1 provides the most support through repetition of high-frequency words, light text, predictable sentence patterns, and strong visual support.

Level 2 offers early readers a bit more challenge through varied simple sentences, increased text load, and less repetition of high-frequency words.

Level 3 advances early-fluent readers toward fluency through increased text and concept load, less reliance on visuals, longer sentences, and more literary language.

Level 4 builds reading stamina by providing more text per page, increased use of punctuation, greater variation in sentence patterns, and increasingly challenging vocabulary.

Level 5 encourages children to move from "learning to read" to "reading to learn" by providing even more text, varied writing styles, and less familiar topics.

Whichever book is right for your reader, Blastoff! Readers are the perfect books to build confidence and encourage a love of reading that will last a lifetime!

This edition first published in 2020 by Bellwether Media, Inc.

No part of this publication may be reproduced in whole or in part without written permission of the publisher. For information regarding permission, write to Bellwether Media, Inc., Attention: Permissions Department, 6012 Blue Circle Drive, Minnetonka, MN 55343.

Library of Congress Cataloging-in-Publication Data

Names: Moening, Kate, author.
Title: Kathleen Kennedy : Movie Producer / by Kate Moening.
Description: Minneapolis, MN : Bellwether Media, Inc., 2020. | Series: Blastoff! Readers : Women Leading the Way | Audience: Ages 5-8. | Audience: Grades K to 3. | Includes bibliographical references and index.
Identifiers: LCCN 2018053556 (print) | LCCN 2018059393 (ebook) | ISBN 9781618916723 (ebook) | ISBN 9781644871003 (hardcover : alk. paper) | ISBN 9781618917232 (paperback : alk. paper) Subjects: LCSH: Kennedy, Kathleen, 1954–Juvenile literature. | Women motion picture producers and directors–United States-Biography–Juvenile literature.
Classification: LCC PN1998.3.K3953 (ebook) | LCC PN1998.3.K3953 M64 2020 (print) | DDC 791.4302/32092 [B] –dc23
LC record available at https://lccn.loc.gov/2018053556

Editor: Al Albertson   Designer: Andrea Schneider

Printed in the United States of America, North Mankato, MN.

Table of Contents

Who Is Kathleen Kennedy?

Kathleen Kennedy is a movie **producer**.

She has produced Indiana Jones and Star Wars **films** and more!

Kathleen on an Indiana Jones set

"THE GREAT THING ABOUT STAR WARS IS IT IS SO **OPTIMISTIC** AND SO **HOPEFUL**." (2015)

Kathleen grew up in Redding, California. She was a leader.

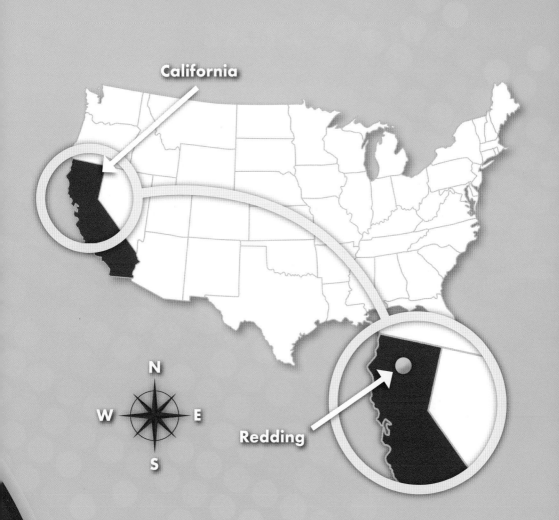

California

Redding

N
W E
S

In middle school, she was the **quarterback** of the boys' football team!

Getting Her Start

Close Encounters of the Third Kind

In college, Kathleen saw a movie called *Close Encounters of the Third Kind*. It was about **aliens**.

The movie helped Kathleen decide to make films!

Kathleen Kennedy Profile

Birthday: June 5, 1953

Hometown: Redding, California

Industry: film

Education:
- degree in film and telecommunications (San Diego State University)

Influences and Heroes:
- David Lean (director)
- Francis Ford Coppola (director)
- Stanley Kubrick (director)
- François Truffaut (director)
- Federico Fellini (director)

Kathleen became a **camera operator** on a news show.

Later, she met a **director** named Steven Spielberg. He **hired** Kathleen to help him make movies!

camera operator

Kathleen with
Steven Spielberg

Changing the World

Indiana Jones and the Raiders of the Lost Ark

Kathleen helped Steven make the first Indiana Jones movie. People loved it!

Steven believed in Kathleen. He asked her to produce *E.T. the Extra-Terrestrial.*

E.T. the Extra-Terrestrial

Kathleen started a film **company** with her future husband and Steven.

They amazed people with *Jurassic Park*. They used **special effects** no one had seen before!

Kathleen and Steven on the set of *Jurassic Park*

"HAVE A POINT OF VIEW AND HAVE SOMETHING TO SAY. THAT IS IMPORTANT IF YOU ARE A FILMMAKER OR ARTIST." (2017)

Kathleen and her husband, Frank

Kathleen began producing new Star Wars movies in 2012.

Kathleen with the actors of
Star Wars: The Force Awakens

Kathleen on a Star Wars set

She knew they needed **meaningful** characters and a great story.

Kathleen is planning more Star Wars films for a new **generation** of movie watchers.

Kathleen Kennedy Timeline

1981   Kathleen, her future husband Frank, and Steven form the production company Amblin Entertainment

1982   Kathleen produces her first film, *E.T. The Extra-Terrestrial*

1991   Kathleen and Frank form the Kennedy/Marshall Company

2012   George Lucas asks Kathleen to take over Lucasfilm Ltd. and the Star Wars movies

She is also producing an Indiana Jones movie for 2021!

Kathleen wants movies to **represent** many people. She hires women and people of color.

She also wants more women to make films. She believes movies are for everyone!

Star Wars: The Force Awakens

"BELIEVE AND SET YOUR SIGHTS ON THE FACT THAT **YOU CAN DO IT.**" (2015)

Glossary

aliens—beings that come from or live somewhere other than the planet Earth

camera operator—the person who records during the filming of a movie or show

company—a group that makes, buys, or sells goods for money

director—a person who leads people making a movie or show

films—movies

generation—a group of people born and living during the same time

hired—chose a person for a job

meaningful—important and full of feelings

producer—the person in charge of making and getting money for a movie

quarterback—the player in football who leads the team's attempts to score

represent—to show

special effects—images or sounds that are created to show something that is not there; the *Jurassic Park* dinosaurs were created using special effects.

To Learn More

AT THE LIBRARY

Bell, Samantha. *You Can Work in Movies*. North Mankato, Minn.: Capstone Press, 2019.

Farrell, Dan, and Donna Bamford. *The Movie-Making Book: Skills and Projects to Learn and Share*. Chicago, Ill.: Chicago Review Press, 2017.

Grabham, Tim. *Video Ideas*. New York, N.Y.: DK Publishing, 2018.

ON THE WEB

FACTSURFER

Factsurfer.com gives you a safe, fun way to find more information.

1. Go to www.factsurfer.com.

2. Enter "Kathleen Kennedy" into the search box and click Q.

3. Select your book cover to see a list of related web sites.

Index